LIGHTHOUSES OF THE WORLD

John Batchelor

DOVER PUBLICATIONS, INC.
Mineola, New York

Note

Around the world, lighthouses have become more than just a blinking light in the distance. For many, they have come to symbolize hope and safety to those who have weathered storms—both literal and figurative. Though often picturesque against their coastal backdrops, lighthouses perform crucial functions that go beyond their photogenic appearance. Their lanterns, horns, antennas, and technology all contribute toward man's continuous efforts to survive the worst of nature's fury. Many lighthouse keepers and builders risked their lives so that others may be safe—and this strength is reflected in the very nature of the unyielding towers that they helped to raise and maintain. Though some of the lighthouses are no longer standing or operational, all of the ones shown here have served the world by offering protection to seafarers across the centuries. This book depicts—in chronological order—a variety of lighthouses and lightships from every region of the world.

Bibliographical Note

Lighthouses of the World is a new work, first published by Dover Publications, Inc., in 2005.

DOVER *Pictorial Archive* SERIES

International Standard Book Number: 0-486-43685-3

Manufactured in the United States of America
Dover Publications, Inc., 31 East 2nd Street, Mineola, N.Y. 11501

Alexandria, Egypt. One of the Seven Wonders of the World, the Pharos (lighthouse) of Alexandria was the tallest building on earth during its time, and a structure of aesthetic and scientific interest. Though it no longer stands, there are several surviving accounts which provide a reasonably accurate history of the lighthouse. Built of stone and marble, it was erected in approximately 280 B.C. on the small island of Pharos, in the city of Alexandria on the Mediterranean Sea. Mirrors placed around the top of the tower enhanced the lantern's power at night, and served during the day to reflect sunlight signals to approaching ships. A series of earthquakes destroyed the Pharos in the early 1300s; the depiction shown here is based on theoretical drawings by historians.

Dover, United Kingdom. Maritime commerce was one of the main sources of wealth for the Roman Empire, prompting leaders to invest much in port facilities and improvements in navigation. One important expenditure was a pharos (lighthouse) overlooking the Strait of Dover, the narrowest part of the English Channel. Erected between A.D. 50 and 100, the lighthouse guided ships across the twenty-one miles between Gaul (now known as France) and present-day Britain. Constructed of local flint and standing approximately eighty feet tall, the tower had its first four stories built by the Romans, with the fifth and topmost added in medieval times. The tower was likely lit with coal or wood fires that burned in the top portion. Perched high up on the famous white cliffs that were an important strategic location during the kingdom's war-torn history, the pharos stands on what is now the grounds of Dover Castle, which was built as a stronghold against invasion.

Genoa, Italy. One of the tallest active lighthouses in the world, this structure was built on the shores of Genoa, an important port city for Italy. Genoa has long been a hub for the Mediterranean shipping industry, and counts Christopher Columbus as one of its sons. Columbus's uncle, Antonio, was one of the keepers of the original lighthouse at Genoa, known as Lanterna or the Faro Tower. It was built during the twelfth century on the western end of the port, first lit by wood fires and then by oil lamps. In the early 1500s, the lighthouse was damaged by artillery fire and reconstructed in 1543. The 200-foot-tall tower is made of brick, and stands on a rocky promontory known as Capo di Faro (Lighthouse Cape). This illustration is based on a 1854 painting showing the nineteenth-century stone and terra cotta buildings gathered below the tower, rather than the modern structures that surround it today.

Damietta, Egypt. Though it no longer exists, the lighthouse at Damietta was erected close to the present-day entrance of the Suez Canal, which links the Mediterranean and Red seas. Only a few sketches of the tower have survived, drawn by travelers making their way to nearby Alexandria on the Nile delta. The lanterns, which were probably lifted to the top of the tower with a lever known as a *vippefyr,* had oil-fueled lights that were capable of being seen at a distance of twenty miles, depending on the brightness of the flames. Constructed over a span of six years, the lighthouse is reputed to have stood until at least the seventeenth century. This illustration is based on a drawing made in 1678.

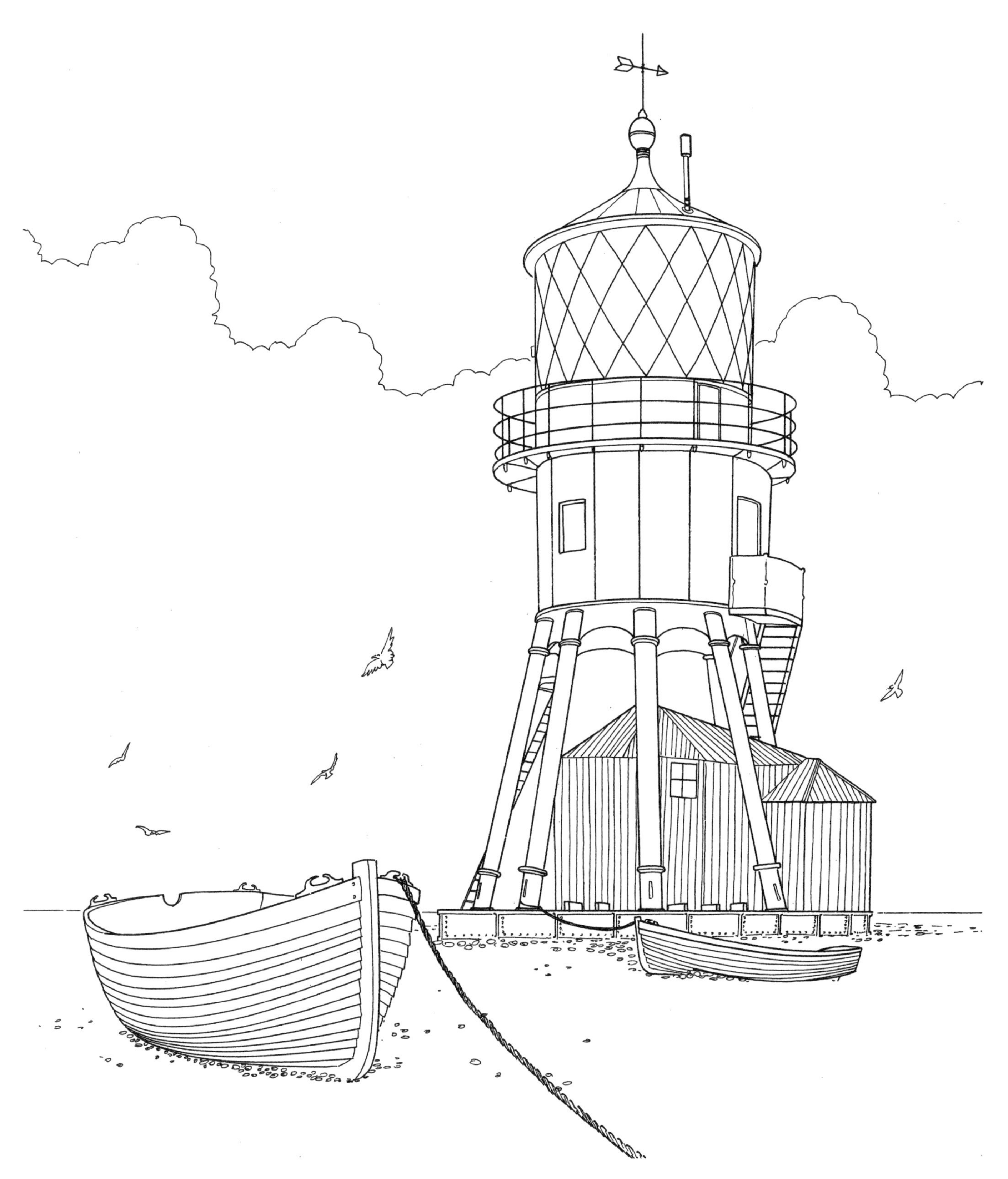

Lowestoft, United Kingdom. Responding to the complaints from merchants and mariners about lost ships and cargo on the east coast of England, Trinity House (a U.K. maritime organization) built two lighthouses at Lowestoft in 1609. In 1676, one of the towers was moved from the beach to a cliff in order to be visible from farther distances, and was thereafter known as the High Light. The Low Light, which stayed on the beach, was discontinued in 1706 due to the encroachment of the ocean, much to the dismay of sailors. Twenty-four years later, it was rebuilt as a moveable tower (shown here) in order to accommodate the changing tide patterns and the movements of the nearby Stamford Channel. The High Light was replaced by a more modern structure in 1874, and was fully automated in 1995. With the disappearance of the Stamford Channel by the early 1900s, the Low Light ceased operation in 1923.

Lisbon, Portugal. The Bugio took over fifty-six years to be constructed, due to the hazardous conditions for the workers. Located just south of the capital, the reef on which the tower and surrounding fort stands becomes flooded at high tide. During the laying of the foundation, only small boats conveying even smaller amounts of stone were able to navigate the shallow waters to drop their loads. Finished in 1775, it has undergone many modifications since then, and is now fully automated. Over the centuries, the structure was nearly demolished by fierce waves, but a protective reef was later built as a barrier to further damage.

Algiers, Algeria. More like a fort than a lighthouse, the tower at the Algiers port was part of the overall defense system of the coast. The illustration shows embrasures built around the base of the lighthouse, equipped with cannon holes in case of an attack. The Algerian mariners were adept at looting any European ships that were unfortunate enough to pass through the port, a practice that was particularly prevalent in the early sixteenth century during the time of Barbarossa, who gave his name to the sinister Barbary pirates. The lighthouse was, in fact, built to facilitate this unsavory trade by guiding the privateers (government-commissioned pirates) safely back to the port. Though started in the late 1600s, the structure was not completed until 1776. Lit with coal, wood, or oil fires, the light from this tower was only visible for five miles, but far enough to serve its unscrupulous purpose.

Cloch Point, Scotland. Completed in 1797 after three years of construction, the Cloch Point lighthouse benefited from the innovative oil-lamp technology that had been recently implemented at the nearby Cumbrae Lighthouse, erected in 1793. Thomas Smith, an Edinburgh lampmaker, had submitted his theories on parabolic reflectors in lanterns to the regional trustees, and was subsequently hired to put the lighthouse into operation. However, with the trustees under financial hardship, the amount of fuel for the lamps and the salary of the lighthouse keeper were considered expendable. The keeper was forced to take on an additional job as a ship pilot to supplement his meager income of thirty guineas a year.

Riga, Latvia. One of many lighthouses lining the Baltic Sea, this lighthouse stands at the mouth of the Daugava River at Riga, Latvia's capital city. Made of stone, it replaced a wooden lighthouse that had been destroyed by war-related attacks in 1808–1809. With the region under Russian control when the lighthouse was built, a crowned letter "A" was placed on the lighthouse as a tribute to Czar Alexander I. An unusual feature of the tower is the arrangement of horizontal spans, on which were hung large orbs of brass or copper to signal the state of the treacherous tides of the Gulf of Riga. By this time, the lanterns of the lighthouse were fitted with silver-plated copper reflectors, and fueled with hemp or turnip oil.

Cape Town, South Africa. The Green Point Lighthouse, built in 1824, was the first lighthouse to be erected on the southern coast of Africa. It directs traffic around the Cape of Good Hope, which is an integral route for the worldwide shipping industry. In 1865, it was raised to its present height, enabling the light to be visible for twenty-three miles. The tower is painted with red and white bands, which make a distinctive contrast against the blue waters of the Indian Ocean.

Key Biscayne, United States. The Cape Florida tower was erected at the entrance to Biscayne Bay in 1825, and is known as Florida's oldest lighthouse. At sixty-five feet tall, the tower was specified to be built with solid brick walls, but later investigations found that the unscrupulous contractors left them hollow. One of this lighthouse's many distinctions is its role as a battlefront when it was attacked by Seminoles in 1836. During the siege, in which the assistant keeper was wounded and his servant killed, it suffered damage that was not repaired for another ten years. The lighthouse underwent a series of renovations, closings, and relightings until it was extinguished in 1878 in favor of a new reef light on nearby Fowey Rocks. One hundred years later, in 1978, it was updated and returned to active status by the United States Coast Guard. The keeper's house is now a museum.

Europa Point, Gibraltar. Guarding the Strait of Gibraltar, which links the Mediterranean Sea with the Atlantic Ocean, this lighthouse was built in 1841 at the southernmost point of Europe. The tower, picturesquely located between the famed Rock of Gibraltar and the rugged regions of North Africa, sports a distinctive red band around its middle. It stands sixty-two feet tall, and is about 160 feet above sea level. The light, which was fully automated in 1994, still retains an attendant to handle the rare emergency. It can be seen up to twenty-one miles on a clear day—a key feature for a passageway that presently accommodates a quarter of the global shipping industry.

Shetland Islands, United Kingdom. Situated at the northernmost point of the British Isles, the Muckle Flugga tower stands on a rocky outcrop off the coast of Scotland. With a sixty-six-foot-high tower putting the light at 280 feet above sea level, the beacon shines to a distance of twenty-five miles. Because the jagged terrain prohibited any wheeled carts, construction in 1854 forced workers to pick their way through the crags on foot, carrying every pound of the 120 tons of material on their backs. Despite its imposing height and strong iron framework, the tower seemed to be in danger of being overwhelmed by the enormous Arctic-born waves that often engulfed it. However, though the wooden doors might be smashed open by the water pressure, the iron pedestal and three-and-a-half-foot-thick walls have withstood the waves to this day. The keepers, who had a lonely job tending to the isolated lighthouse, were relieved of their duty in 1995, when Muckle Flugga became fully automated.

West Quoddy Head, United States. The picturesque red and white bands of this lighthouse, located in Maine at the easternmost point of the United States, make it a favorite subject of photographers. It is also the northernmost lighthouse in the country, standing near the Canadian border. The first tower was built in 1808, by order of Thomas Jefferson, to guide boats along the Quoddy Roads. Besides maintaining the lantern, the keeper was also require to ring the fog bell when there was poor visibility on the water—a task that earned the 1827 keeper an extra sixty dollars per year. The present structure, which stands forty-nine feet high, was erected in 1858, along with an adjacent keeper's house. The light was fully automated in 1988, over the objections of the unfortunate keeper.

Isle of Wight, United Kingdom. To protect sailors from a hazardous group of jagged rocks known as the Needles, the original lighthouse was built in 1786 on a cliff overlooking the rocks. Veiled in mist and fog, that light proved to be too high to be of real service to ships. Thus, in 1859, the present lighthouse was built on the outermost rock of the grouping, which gave sailors a clear indication of the danger area. Rising 109 feet high, the granite tower is painted red and white, and is equipped with a helicopter-landing pad. The Isle of Wight is the home of Cowes Week, the world-famous annual sailing regatta that was first held in 1826.

Bay of Biscay, Spain. Built in 1864, this lighthouse was just one of the dozens that line the treacherous southern coast of the Bay of Biscay. This region, which comprises Spain's northern border, is known by mariners for its sudden storms and rocky shores. No longer operational, this lighthouse is mainly visited by ambitious hikers, as the only approach to the tower involves the negotiation of 682 steep, crumbling steps down a cliff. When the light was in use, every item that the keeper needed would be carried down the steps by a courier, who would then have to make the grueling return trip back up the cliff. Though wooden landings were built at the base of the cliff, these were dashed to pieces so often that further construction attempts were soon abandoned.

Assateague Island, United States. Though a lighthouse was built in 1833 on Assateague Island, it proved to be too short and dim to properly guide sailors between Cape Charles in Virginia and Delaware's Cape Henlopen. At only forty-five feet high, and with only eleven lamps, the stone tower was a failure. On the day before the outbreak of the Civil War, Congress finally authorized the funds for a replacement, but those plans were hastily shelved until the war was over. In 1867, the new brick lighthouse was finally completed, standing at 142 feet tall, and fitted with a light that could be seen for eighteen miles. Automated in 1963, the photogenic red-and-white-striped tower stands inside what is now the Chincoteague National Wildlife Refuge, an area famous for its wild ponies. Though it was initially built alongside the coast, the lighthouse is now five miles inland, due to the shifting shorelines of the island.

Brittany, France. Erected off the coast of Finistère, Le Four lighthouse has been widely photographed for its stoic resistance against the gigantic waves of the Atlantic Ocean. It was built in 1874 with interlocking blocks of stone, which have held up admirably against the powerful tides. However, the shock of the strongest waves has been known to propel the lighthouse's furniture across the room. For over one hundred years, workers had to be transferred to the lighthouse by winches from their boats, as they were never able to dock their vessels on the tumultuous shore. In 1993, the light, which rises 102 feet above sea level, was automated. In especially severe storms, the entire structure disappears in bursting waves that send white water high above the beacon.

Selangor, Malaysia. Though no longer functional, One Fathom Bank Lighthouse played a crucial role in the development of the Strait of Malacca as an important shipping thoroughfare. Built in 1874, its unusual design consists of an octagonal base built on pilings, on which was raised a skeleton framework that holds the lantern. The lighthouse was operational for an impressive 125 years, before it was replaced with a new lighthouse of the same name. The Strait of Malacca is the second busiest shipping lane in the world, after the Strait of Dover in the United Kingdom. It connects the Indian and China seas, and about 200 ships pass through its waters daily.

Bremerhaven, Germany. Situated where the Weser River empties into the North Sea, Bremerhaven was quickly developing into an important port city in the mid-nineteenth century, impeded only by the treacherous sandbars and shoals. Though a lighthouse was the obvious answer, it seemed impossible to erect one on the shifting sand. A reputable German engineering firm was asked to find a solution, which resulted in the idea of a caisson—a large steel barrel to be sunk deep in the sand as the foundation for the tower. Theory proved easier than practice, however, as a series of mishaps and delays forced the engineers to scrap the first caisson, which was circular in shape. The next rendition was oval, measuring sixty-one feet high and forty-six feet around at its widest point. Many powerful tugs towed the structure to the proper location, where it was finally sunk and reinforced. The Rothersand lighthouse was soon erected on top of the caisson, and the light became operational in 1885.

Point St. George, United States. Following such disasters as the 1865 wreck of the USS *Brother Jonathan*, in which 200 people perished, government officials finally began plans to erect a lighthouse on the fatal reefs of St. George in northern California in 1882. After a prolonged delay due to lack of federal funding, work began in earnest in 1887. The contractors faced the daunting task of carving into the rock and reefs in order to lay the foundation, which was constructed of granite and concrete. Fierce storms and high winds buffeted the site; one worker was even swept away by the powerful waves of the ocean. The square granite tower was finally lit in 1892, although the tragedies did not cease. Numerous injuries and deaths plagued the lighthouse until 1975, when the U. S. Coast Guard closed it down and instead placed a buoy near the reefs to warn mariners away.

Golden Bay, New Zealand. Located on a sixteen-mile sand-spit on the northern coast of South Island, the Farewell Spit light was a welcome relief to mariners who had long feared the dangerous sandbars along the coast. The first version, built in 1870, was rather primitive—a lantern perched on wooden stilts on the beach. After decay and erosion ate into the wood, the current orange-and-white steel structure was erected in 1897. The windy conditions and ever-present sand made life difficult for both the keepers, who had to constantly shovel sand out of their house, and the contractors. While constructing the lighthouse, workers discovered that a large heap of bricks had disappeared under the sand after an evening storm. Though they dug around repeatedly for a whole day, they never found the bricks, and were forced to halt work until a new shipment arrived.

San Francisco, United States. Deep water and unstable terrain were problems for many communities where a light was needed, as well as expense and impracticality. Some, such as San Francisco, opted instead to anchor lightships at treacherous points. These boats, equipped with tall masts fitted with lanterns, were often in danger themselves, having to be anchored in place during the severest of weather. Crew members suffered through months-long stints on lightships, often plagued with boredom, discomfort, and inadequate supplies. Lightship #70 was commissioned in 1898 to mark the entrance to the San Francisco Bay, and was anchored for thirty-two years by the Golden Gate Bridge. The vessel was retired in 1930, and afterward was used by a cannery before it was wrecked in Alaska in 1941.

Victoria, Australia. In 1854, a privately established light was erected on a metal tower at Point Lonsdale to guide ships into Port Phillip. That first light was replaced in 1863 by a wooden structure, which had previously been used in nearby Queenscliff before a stone lighthouse was built there. The third and present tower, depicted here, was built in 1901. Made of concrete, it stands sixty-nine feet high and is one of the dwindling number of lighthouses still maintained by keepers. The signal station around the base of the tower was built in 1950, and houses five keepers who keep a constant twenty-four-hour vigil over the bay.

West Cork, Ireland. Poignantly known as the "Teardrop of Ireland," Fastnet Rock is a lonely island off the coast of Cape Clear, and was the final sight of home for the Irish who emigrated to America. A bleak and dangerous outcropping, Fastnet was necessarily fitted with a cast-iron lighthouse, erected in 1854. Though the tower itself was strong, the high cliffs on which it stood were not. Crashing waves continually clawed at the boulders, in some instances ripping tons of rock away with each tide and hurling them back at the tower. Though the lighthouse escaped major damage, plans were begun in 1891 to replace it with a stronger structure. For the next fifteen years, designs were drafted and construction took place among harsh and unpredictable conditions. In 1906, the graceful white granite tower was completed, standing 177 feet high, with a light that can be seen twenty-seven miles away.

Queen Charlotte Islands, Canada. Langara Island lies in the northern Pacific Ocean, and comprises one of the islands in the remote Queen Charlotte chain in British Columbia. With the advancement of a railroad to nearby Prince Rupert, it was inevitable that there would be a growth in shipping in that region. A stately lighthouse, complete with buttresses, was designed in 1908. Construction was problematic in the harsh conditions of the region, especially because the island was nearly impossible to reach in inclement weather. The contractors, faced with challenging work and the monotony of an isolated lifestyle, demanded more money and were refused. Funding was on a tight leash, and even necessities such as horses for towing were questioned. Despite the hardships, Langara Lighthouse was completed in 1913, and still functions today. The white concrete tower, topped with a red lantern, stands eighty-two feet tall.

Vancouver, Canada. The first light established at Brockton Point was rather primitive, consisting of several red and white lanterns strung together and tied to a mast in 1890. The light, which marked the entrance into Coal Harbour, failed to adequately house the keeper, who obstinately built his own rickety shack out of driftwood instead. It was only until the dukes of Cornwall and York were due for a royal visit to the park in which the light stood, that the eyesore was removed and a real home built for the keeper. It was replaced in 1915 by the current structure, which is painted white with a single red horizontal band and is still operational today. The arch at the base of the tower was intended to hold a boathouse, but the bay's currents are too violent to allow prolonged docking.

Murano, Italy. Since the thirteenth century, the island of Murano has been hailed as the center for glassblowing artistry. Though the industry started in nearby Venice, the artisans and foundries were moved to Murano in 1291 due to the danger of fire and smoke to the wooden buildings of the city. The lighthouse, known as the Faro di Murano, guards the entrance to the Venice Lagoon from the Mediterranean Sea, where sandbanks make navigation difficult. The tower, built in 1924, is constructed of white stone, striped with two bold black bands.

Cape Reinga, New Zealand. Perched on one of the northernmost points of New Zealand, the Cape Reinga Lighthouse welcomes sailors arriving via the Tasman Sea and Pacific Ocean. The diminutive white concrete tower is only thirty-three feet high, but due to its location on a high cliff, its light actually shines 541 feet above sea level and is visible for twenty-six miles. It was completed in 1941 and was one of the last lighthouses to have a keeper, being fully automated in 1987. According to Maori legend, recently departed spirits go in search of their original homeland by climbing down the cliff and over the water below, which is appropriately named "Spirits Bay."

Kent, United Kingdom. The South Goodwin Lightship met a tragic end in its duty to guide sailors through the precarious Strait of Dover. On November 27, 1954, a fierce storm raged through the area, bringing with it winds that gusted up to eighty miles an hour. A coastguard on shore noticed that night that the light from the ship was not visible, though the mist and rain might have accounted for its absence. The South Goodwin had not issued any distress calls or fired any flares, so there seemed to be no need for alarm. Shortly afterward, however, the East Goodwin lightship reported her comrade vessel drifting by. The South Goodwin, which had been anchored on the eastern end of the Goodwin Sands, had broken from her moorings and capsized in the water, killing all seven members of her crew. Miraculously, an American birdwatcher onboard the South Goodwin clung to the side of the ship for hours until rescued by helicopter. The sad fate of the lightship underscores the grave risks taken by all lighthouse keepers and contractors who have worked to provide safe passage for others.